Old NEWTONGRANGE, GOREBRIDGE &

by
Rhona Wilson

GENERAL VIEW, NEWTONGRANGE.

This 1930s picture shows the rather bleak and uniform rows of a traditional mining town made up of streets which weren't so much named as hastily numbered; First Street, Second Street and so on. Still, when they were built they were considered a model example. Before the mid-nineteenth century many collier's homes were just temporary shacks put up beside the pit.

© Stenlake Publishing 1997
First Published in the United Kingdom, 1997
by Stenlake Publishing Ltd.
Telephone: 01290 551122
www.stenlake.co.uk

ISBN 1 872074 93 6

In the late 1870s Britain's coal industry was in depression but the mines at Newtongrange and Rosewell prospered quietly. This continued uneventfully until the Newbattle and Whitehill Collieries amalgamated to form the Lothian Coal Company in 1890. Over the next five years the LCC sunk the mammoth Victoria Pit which made Newtongrange the centre of mining in the region, resulting in a period of massive development. Around 1890 the village population was about nine hundred. A decade later it had swollen to almost two and a half thousand with clubs, bands and societies springing up to support it. The coal company had to supply houses for the floods of incomers and did so by being involved in new building companies. Over fifteen years the Newbattle and Whitehill Building Company put up hundreds of homes.

Introduction

Now a picturesque hamlet, in danger of being subsumed by its neighbour Dalkeith, Newbattle was the original Midlothian mining village. The monks of Newbattle Abbey discovered coal there as early as the thirteenth century, although at first they used it to keep their saltpans bubbling at Preston. Coal was considered an unhealthy fuel at the time and there was little domestic demand for it. By the 1530s superstitions had dissipated and their 'black gold' provided the monks with a valuable export to trade with the surrounding villages.

During the turmoil of the Reformation a few decades later, Mark Ker the 'Abbot' hastily gave up Catholicism to retain the Abbey lands. His son became the first Earl of Lothian and the family continued to manage the mines directly for another three centuries. Initially mining methods were haphazard. Shallow pits were worked and abandoned if structural problems developed; it was easy enough to start another. Escalating demand brought more structure to the industry - witness the 1606 Act which made all miners serfs in a bid to guarantee a workforce.

But it was the industrialisation of the nineteenth century which brought massive change to Midlothian. When the Edinburgh & Dalkeith Railway arrived in 1829 it brought with it access to markets which were previously inaccessible. Financed by a group of interested parties, the Marquis of Lothian built a viaduct to extend the line to his Midlothian coalfields. Rosewell's Whitehill pit, run by the Ramsays, also benefited as did Dundas pits in Gorebridge. The entire district was transformed as a result, in particular Newtongrange and Rosewell which were mere hamlets before. Gorebridge was a metropolis by comparison but, at that time, eked a living mainly from the gunpowder mill at Stobmills. Mined casually for years, its mining industry didn't develop properly until it got a railway station around 1847.

From this point coal travelled through Newtongrange by rail instead of through Newbattle by cart heralding a reversal of fortune for the two villages, the latter slowly withering away as its passing trade disappeared. By contrast a decade later Newtongrange was chosen to house the miners flooding in to work at the pits with a brickworks set up to facilitate this. Rosewell had grown big enough to merit a church thirty years later and Nitten had its own gas works.

In 1890 Whitehill and Newbattle Collieries amalgamated to form the Lothian Coal Company and spent the next five years sinking the massive Victoria Pit. Once again massive development took place to house the incoming miners, particularly in Newtongrange. Entertainment facilities sprung up to service the growing communities with Miners' Institutes being organised as standard. The collieries prospered through the early decades of twentieth century until the mines were worked out around the fifties and sixties. The mighty Victoria shut in 1961 as did many others, devastating the mining-dependent villages.

'Ghost Town' became the complacent label for the villages left behind as people moved away to find work. Large numbers of homes were boarded up and some villages complained about infestations of rats. Shops closed down and the railtracks which had once precipitated the coal boom were slowly removed as freight dried up. Newtongrange, the most successful mining village, had the most to lose. In the early eighties it was the subject of a BBC documentary titled 'The Town that Nobody Wants', which focused on the plans to demolish it.

In recent years the fortunes of these Midlothian villages have been mixed. Newbattle is picturesque, suggesting a romantic past which doesn't include mining. Rosewell and Gorebridge, on the other hand, are obviously old mining towns with little other identity. The former is a one street settlement whereas Gorebridge's old habit of swallowing up smaller villages seems to have resulted in a community strangely disparate.

Of them all, Newtongrange has proved itself the survivor.

The dread days of the seventies seem to have acted as a kick up the backside for the Newtongrange villagers, who appear feisty to say the least. The rebirth of the Lady Victoria as the Scottish Mining Museum was a major factor in renewing self-esteem, likewise the pit wheels and mining statues scattered around its streets act as a constant reminder of a heritage, not just a lost industry.

Victoria Pit Bottom, NEWTONGRANGE.

Going down this Pit on Saturday week. How would you like to go.? I shall tell you how I enjoyed it later on. Yours. Effie

The carts of coal pictured here were transported by horse but women were often used to carry coal. In 1812 Robert Bald wrote a shocking survey which took a look at 'The Condition of Women who Carry Coals'. The most extreme form of this practice was when women and children had to transport coal from the wall face to the pithead. Around the time Bald wrote his report women were banned from carrying out the job in Glasgow but Lothian was known for its tough conditions.

'The Lady', as she was affectionately known, was one of the deepest mines in the country and produced around forty million tons of coal before her demise. Over her lifespan she went through her fair share of managers. A Mr Morrison was one of the first gaffers around the 1890s and chose to live at Millhill House. Mungo MacKay who succeeded him was made of sterner stuff. He moved into a house opposite the pit to keep a closer eye on its comings and goings; lauded as a technical genius he was also carefully considered to be an absolute dictator by his employees.

The houses on the right originally belonged to the foremen and heads of department from the Newbattle Paper Mills. After the mills closed they were taken over first by the LCC and later by the National Coal Board who had to pay rent to the Marquis of Lothian trustees and sublet. Some time later the Coal Board went to court in an attempt to stop being the 'unwilling supporters' of fourteen families who lived there in condemned houses, rent-free. Their argument went along the lines that they should never have taken over the houses anyway because they weren't occupied by colliery workers. It was all a mistake because the Coal Board had had so much property to sort out! There are no arguments now as they've been completely demolished.

Old Gates, the bottom end of the village, around 1906. Before the 1890s the Newbattle Paper Mill was a big source of employment for the surrounding villages with Newtongrange no exception. The mills were set up in the 1790s and taken over later by the Craig family who started their lucrative paper making around the turn of the century. The Craigs had a ten year long dispute over rent with their landlord the Marquis. Unable to come to an agreement they decided to give up the lease in the 1890s but ended up in court over that too. The Craigs wanted to take their gasworks and water fixtures with them to their other works in Caldercruix but the Marquis claimed they belonged to him. Whatever the outcome of the court case the real losers were the mill employees. In 1890 workers living in company houses were give four days notice to quit their homes.

MAIN STREET, NEWTONGRANGE

The bottom of the village looking a bit sprucer around 1918. This part of the village has since changed only superficially although the gas works' chimney, set up in the 1870s to provide lighting, has gone.

MAIN ST, NEWTONGRANGE.

The Dean Tavern on the left-hand corner was set up by the directors of the LCC in the late 1890s as a Gothenburg experiment. Gothenburgs infiltrated east coast mining villages throughout the late nineteenth and early twentieth century as a result of trading contacts with Sweden. They were a style of pub developed by the Sweden temperance movement to encourage sobriety. Profits were limited for shareholders and money raised from the bar was ploughed back into the community. They provided colliery managers with a means of controlling their miners' drinking habits and at the same time getting them to pay for local facilities. The Dean was first housed in the three cottages seen here before a new building was put up around 1910. Today the Dean still has its horseshoe bar, airy internal archway and a houseful of local worthies - definitely a pub full of character!

INSTITUTE AND MAIN STREET, NEWTONGRANGE

The Evening News reported a big dispute at the miner's institute, pictured on the left, in the mid-1990s. Opened in 1911 through contributions from the Lady Vic workers, Nitten's institute faced closure at around the same time as Rosewells. However, a local businessman stepped in to pay off its debts and the building is still open. It is known as the 'Top Club' because of its location at the top end of the village. Just along from it is the Newbattle Pool.

Main Street. Newtongrange.   M. 161

Newtongrange Picture Palace (on the left) was financed by the Dean and opened in 1915 screening 'Out of the Depths'. From being a large, prosperous community Newtongrange itself crashed to the depths once the Vic was worked out in the early 1980s. Almost one in ten homes were boarded up by the time people had left to find work. Shops closed, the empty homes were infested with rats - there was even talk of demolishing the old miners' rows. A 1983 BBC documentary about Nitten entitled 'The Village that Nobody Wants' said it all. But in bloody minded fashion Newtongrange took its bad publicity and used it to survive with a decade's worth of improvements. Castle Rock Housing Association finally decided they did want to renovate the houses, the Vic was converted into a museum in 1984 and the village even held an exhibition on itself in the community centre!

Picture Palace, Newtongrange

One of the most noticeable changes to Newtongrange has been its street furniture. As soon as you get near the Vic the references to mining begin. A concrete overpass at the museum has (pasted on) miners 'walking' through it and several pit wheels painted bright red are strewn about the village. Most bizarre, however, are the pagoda bus shelters on Main Street. Although they look like bandstands, they are crowned by golden canaries, apparently to symbolise the bird cages miners took down the pit to test for gas. Nice thought I'm sure, but they are more often used as toilets...

Newtongrange House (near the Galadale area) was the neo-baronial residence of 'Cocky' John Romans, a consultant engineer who didn't have to rely on the pits for an income. When the Marquis began to expand his coal interests and brought more miners into the district, Romans was keen to cash in by building homes for rent. The Marquis, not amused because he'd built some himself, tried to hinder the other's plans by closing ancient rights of way. This meant access to Romans' building was poor and he retaliated by taking the Marquis to court. In an infamous case he proved the Marquis wrong and crowed about if for ever afterwards, even publishing a book of the court case for his friends. Later, when he was chairman of the School Board, Romans was still trying to get at his old rival demanding he be kicked off the board for bad attendance at meetings.

NEWTONGRANGE STATION.

Newtongrange Station, like the other stations in the area, became an uneconomic indulgence when the mines were worked out and the population dropped. By the early 1980s the cleared site was being used as an unofficial dump, occasionally getting blitzed as a school environmental project.

Bowling Green looking towards Roman Camp, Newtongrange.

Nitten's bowling green arrived courtesy of early profits from The Dean. The Roman Camp mentioned in the postcard refers to the one supposedly on Camp Hill. Many such archaeological discoveries in the past were labelled 'Roman' on little evidence and it seems more likely that the camp was used by Scots themselves to guard against invaders. A later legend attached to the area was that of Camp Meg. This eccentric refugee arrived in the late eighteenth century on the run after shooting her neighbour. She took up residence at the Camp's West Stone House, dressed like a man, and worked a variety of tasks to scrape a living; ad hoc vet, cutting whins, casting drains. Rumoured to be a witch because of her singular independence she wasn't popular with the female population of the district and when she died (around the 1820s) eight men alone attended her funeral at Newbattle Church.

Newtongrange Brass Band was founded in 1893, paid for by volunteer donations from the village miners. The band employed a professional conductor. LCC even made it lucrative for potential players to settle in Newtongrange by providing them with houses. In 1905 the group was elevated into a silver band and continued for twenty odd years until it had a dispute with its new administrators (Newbattle Miner's Welfare Committee) and broke up. It was restarted in the early thirties but never resumed the cushy life it had before. The next few decades saw many financial disputes over things such as uniforms, instruments and maintenance of the band hall. Despite the problems the band has survived until the nineties albeit in a different form. Previously financed by the union, the band found themselves penniless after a disagreement in 1985. Commercial sponsors stepped in, however, and the band is now called the Scottish Brewers Silver Band.

Co-ops began to appear after the end of the Napoleonic wars around the 1820s. Gorebridge Co-op was set up in Herrin' Row in the 1860s and opened its first branch in Newtongrange's Station Road in 1908. Although the Co survived as a Scotmid supermarket in recent years, the building's future is now doubtful. Taking up only a quarter of the old Co-op building, this was due to close around the time of writing. Other shops in the picture have suffered a similar fate. The pharmacy in the background was a butcher's for a time but is now boarded up and perhaps Station Road's location in a quiet, tucked away cul-de-sac is partly to blame.

CHILDREN'S SEA-SIDE, WELFARE PARK, NEWTONGRANGE.

Welfare Park is to the south of where the original Newtongrange village stood and was marked as wasteground on an early ordnance survey map. Parks such as these were used as 'lungs' for industrial communities who had little chance of getting fresh air or exercise elsewhere. Often they were the focus for community events - Newtongrange's park was the venue for weekly concerts by the village Silver Band.

1996 Bird's Eye View, Gorebridge

Gorebridge is thought to have got its name from the old layout of the village. Settlements were built in a circle with a triangular piece of common ground known as the 'gore' in the middle, in this case in the gorge near the old railway station. An alternative version claimed the bridge over the Gore water was initially named the 'ghober', an old word for the goats that grazed there, 'gore' being a corruption of this instead. Also known as the Borthwick Burn, the Gore water powered a busy flour mill at Catcune.

STOBSMILLS, GOREBRIDGE.

This picture marks the spot between Gorebridge and Stobmills, linked by the bridge. The sharp and narrow bend of the bridge has since been widened and straightened out and the building on the right has gone. Although Gorebridge became a mining village the area developed because of a different industry, the first major gunpowder works in Scotland set up at Stobmills by Hitchener and Hunter in the early 1790s. Some of its production helped sink Napoleon's fleet at the Battle of Trafalgar. Powdermill Brae consisted of company houses and, since there were few shops for the influx of coopers and powdermakers, Gorebridge village was established to provide these. There were many accidents in this dangerous factory with, as a result, eighty orphans in the local schools at one time.

STOBSMILLS. GOREBRIDGE.

Business had begun to flag by the 1850s and the powdermill closed a decade later when one of the main partners, John Caldwell died. One of the other owners, Charles Hitchener, committed suicide and there is an unresolved story about this. He was buried at Dalkeith's St. Nicholas Church, but this parish refused to allow his sister-in-law to put up a memorial stone for him. This could have been because he took his own life but there were also rumours about affairs with his workers' wives. Whatever the reason, Temple Parish Church proved more sympathetic, allowing a memorial stone to be erected on one of its walls in a gesture of defiance to the Dalkeith Kirk Session. The powdermill deteriorated and was felled in the mid-1870s. Powdermill Brae was also eventually demolished and the houses replaced, the Birkenside housing scheme being developed later.

STOBBS MILL GOREBRIDGE.

Taken at the very top end of Stobmills this scene has changed little over the years. Harvieston Villas (later Dewar Villas) at the bottom of the hill on the right marked the foot of Lady Brae. If you continue up the brae you cross what was previously the railway bridge. The North British Railway opened the station in the late 1840s and residents of Gorebridge once set their watches by the Flying Scotsman which passed through the station around ten at night. Today the station buildings and tracks have themselves flown, as if they never existed.

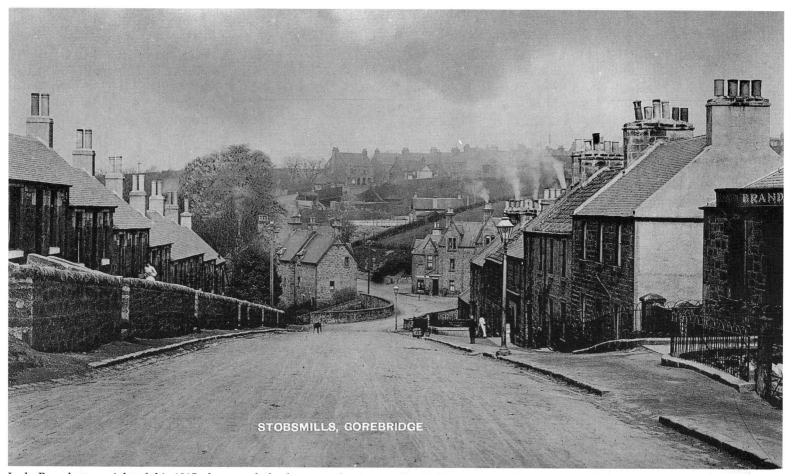

STOBSMILLS, GOREBRIDGE

Lady Brae, bottom right of this 1915 photograph, leads up to what is now Vogrie Country Park. One of the first references to the estate appeared as 'Wogrym', owned by Robert Menzies in the fourteenth century. It was sold to James Dewar around 1719. The estate remained with the Dewars for over two hundred years, the family getting a financial boost when they bought the nearby Stobs estate which proved rich in coal reserves. One of the Dewar family was actually involved in the eighteenth century campaign to change the law which made miners serfs or virtual slaves. Vogrie House was built in the 1870s, ironically at a time when the Dewar family were showing less and less interest in the estate. Rented out at one point, the estate was eventually sold in the 1920s for use as a private nursing home. Midlothian County Council thought about developing the land as a housing scheme, but instead decided to create the present day country estate.

DEWAR VILLAS GOREBRIDGE

Confusion exists over the name Dewar Villas, pictured here around 1906. These were later better known as Harvieston Villas, probably in reference to the nearby Harvieston estate when the Dewar family of Vogrie sold up in the 1920s. The tenement block itself was known as Harvieston Terrace with the 'villas' referring to the top floor which had a separate entrance further up Lady Brae. They were hardly luxurious - no hot water supply and only one outside toilet for the tenants'. Previously owned by the Arniston Coal Company, they were demolished some time before the early 1970s, the stone being used to build an extension for the Stair Arms Hotel. The bridge on the left is now a large concrete affair and the other building near it has also gone. A retaining wall has been built along where the tenements once were.

Gorebridge Main Street developed as an amenity for the workers from the district's collieries and the powdermill. It began to fill up with shops and take the shape it has today around the 1820s. By the early 1850s maps show that the east side was almost complete although there were still gaps to fill in on the west. The shopkeepers first lived above their shops although many on the east side built villas at the foot of their gardens once they'd earned enough. The first building on the left (with the barber's pole) was built in 1894 and is now half boarded up although it has a sign for the Struthers Memorial Church on the front. Opposite, the 'Best Friends' cafe further up was the original police station which has since been replaced by the Bank of Scotland.

In 1840 Gorebridge was still just a few streets. When the North British Railway opened Gorebridge Railway Station in 1847, its development outwith the powdermill began. Robert Dundas of Arniston took advantage by sinking two huge pits; the Emily in the 1850s and the Gore a couple of decades later. Asides from the Catcune flour mill these two became the main employers in the district. By the time the Gore was sunk Gorebridge's population had increased to thousands and the village's consideration of the Police Burgh Act in 1889 shows some evidence of this. The Act was usually engaged when a village had become too big and it gave a board of commissioners the right to raise taxes, manage a police force and run other services. But, this was too expensive and the village instead got itself made into a water supply district, a cheaper way of achieving some sort of aims.

390 Main Street, Gorebridge

The wide sweep of road at the top of Main Street has gone, replaced by some pavement landscaping to narrow it down. New building has taken place round the corner to the left whereas the Gorebridge Inn is still standing. The village went into a decline in the seventies as the pits were closed and demolition began. Labelled as the inevitable 'ghost town', some sixty-six percent of its inhabitants had to travel outside for work. The council's main idea to improve things was the predictable Conservation Order at the end of the decade, to protect the nineteenth century Main Street from unwelcome developments.

3685 Main Street. Gorebridge.

Although, like Rosewell, its buildings remain intact it's difficult to understand why. Decades after the pit closures, people still say that the village is a ghost town and it doesn't seem to have much life about it. Some of the Main Street shops are boarded up and those which are open seem pitifully short of customers.

Main Street looking up towards Newbyres Road. The Fancy Warehouse on the right is the present site of Prestos with a grocer, takeaway and funeral parlour taking up the shops further along. At the back the tenement block once housed a corner shop run by Mr Cranston. It was demolished some time ago before the bowling alley was built.

Newbyres Road, Gorebridge

3687

Newbyres Road pictured around the late 1920s. Newbyres Hall appears on the left.

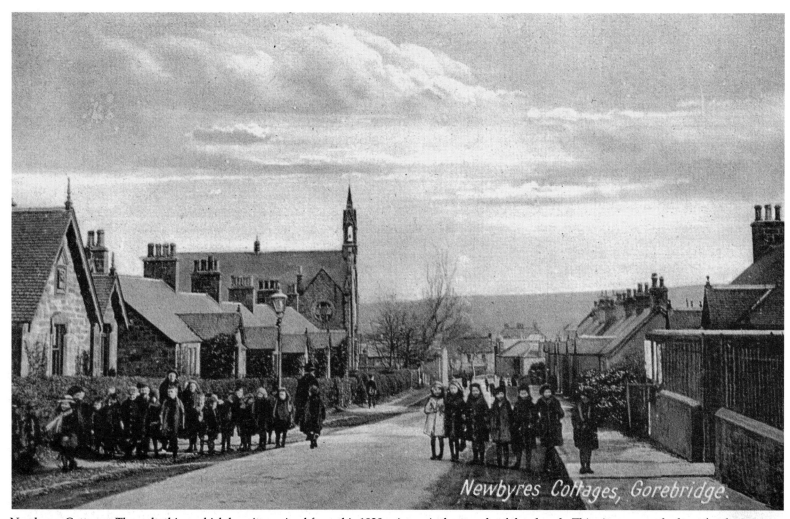

Newbyres Cottages, Gorebridge.

Newbyres Cottages. The only thing which hasn't survived from this 1920s picture is the steeple of the church. This site was marked out for the cottages and library around the late 1880s. Gorebridge's doctor, Dr Inch, lived at Newbyres Cottage which is itself still standing opposite the Health Centre. The first library was established where the centre is, started off in the early nineteenth century with a donation of books from the powdermill doctor. The present library was built further up the street next to the leisure centre.

THE OLD CASTLE GOREBRIDGE

Newbyres Tower was an old keep situated behind Gorebridge's masonic hall. There was a dentists opposite it (later the 'Country Curls' hair salon) and if you were in his chair you got a good view of the tower. Originally L-shaped it dwindled to the ruin pictured here over the years and was mostly demolished sometime in the sixties.

ARNISTON COLLIERY & VILLAGE.

Emily Pit was named after the wife of Robert Dundas, main landowner in Gorebridge. Pictured here around 1910, the brick building in the centre housed its electricity generator, it being one of the first to use electrical pumps. The Dundas family had been mining since the start of the sixteenth century although only on a small scale with a mere ten employees, sinking the bigger pits when the railway was up and running. A joint business venture with the other colliery owners in the district, the railway was organised to open up markets for the Midlothian coalfields as a whole. In the 1830s Arniston Colliery was leased out but Dundas decided to take control and develop it himself.

Emily Pit. Arniston.

R.R.R.
E.

In 1841 Dundas's son banned women and children from working down the pit which pre-empted a ruling by over a year. Alexander Maxton, the colliery manager, gave evidence to the Royal Commission investigating the issue. The miners' homes were kept more comfortable and their wives were no longer demoralised by the back-breaking tasks they had to perform. Boys' bodies weren't strong enough to cope with the work if they were sent down the pit too early. Indeed, they were far more likely to stay at the mine because of the improved home atmosphere and taking on the work when they were physically ready for it. Other commentators stated prudishly that one of the main improvements was that women no longer went down the pub after work with their menfolk!

It's thought that Arniston got its name from a clan who settled there. The original family could have been named Arnoldeson. Completed in the 1750s after thirty years of building, Arnieston House was the Dundas family residence. An orangery was built within the grounds and was one of only three in Scotland at the time. Children were evacuated here from Corstophine during WWII and the mansion house, still standing, was restored some time later.

The cottage behind the 'shaky bridge' in Arniston Glen belonged to the gamekeeper and was known as Joseph's Mill. Within the Glen is King's Cave, named after an eighteenth century smuggler called King who used an area near the cave to rest when he was transporting goods to the coast. Gore Glen Park was created much later from three former bings. It took two years to burn over one hundred tons of colliery waste and plant the thousands of trees required. Lothian Regional Council kindly gifted the park (and of course its maintenance costs) to Midlothian District Council in the early eighties.

FUSHIEBRIDGE

A century ago Fushiebridge in Borthwick was the Post Office hamlet for the surrounding district since the London mail coach changed its horses at Fushie Inn. When the Gorebridge section of the Edinburgh to Hawick railway was built Irish navvies were brought over to finish the job. They lived in turf huts and had extremely bad relations with the natives which resulted in a riot after one particular incident in the 1840s. A squabble started in a pub because some Irishmen refused to give a salesman back a watch. He called the police who jailed the men in question. Drunk and angry they broke out of prison and ran riot, kicking to death a policeman who happened to get in their way. The next day nine hundred incensed locals from the surrounding communities gathered to search for the assailants. In the meantime word had spread to the Irish community in Edinburgh who organised a march to defend their countrymen. In the end forty dragoons had to be called in to sort the mess out.

Around 1910 this group of German gypsies turned up in Gorebridge. Rumoured to be spies amongst locals, they had actually fled from persecution in their own country. Nearby Roslin had a long connection with gypsy visitors going back to mediaeval days. Before the nineteenth century gypsies could be useful to an isolated community, bringing in goods and services difficult to obtain otherwise.

Stobhill Parish Church & School Firman Gorebridge.

Stobhill Church was built in the 1830s and became the parish church some twenty years later. There were several free churches in the surrounding district frequented by miners. Pit workers built two in Gorebridge, one in what became the Masonic Hall and another which ended up as the Struthers Memorial Church.

Newtonloan Hospital. Gorebridge.

Newtonloan was a fever hospital built around 1890 at the instigation of Mr Dundas of Arniston to deal with epidemics. It ran an ambulance waggon and was in an isolated position to provide reasonable quarantine facilities. These days it is an old folks home. In the late 1890s an article entitled "Lunatic at Large" appeared in the Dalkeith Advertiser about a miner causing havoc in Newtongrange. George Davies burst in upon the congregation one Sunday and screamed at them that they were a bunch of "bloody hypocrites". The next couple of days saw him involved in a few street skirmishes which got him thrown into Rosewell Asylum for his trouble.

Whitehill pit was being worked around the mid-1740s although Rosewell didn't become a mining village proper until the advent of the railways. During the eighteenth century miners were still serfs, owned by the mines they worked in, and in 1770 a group of Whitehill miners caused a stir by running away. They got as far as Glasgow before they were caught and sent back under an armed escort. Although Whitehill was owned by the Ramsays it wasn't until Archibald Hood took over that the industry really took off. Hood, originally an employee of the family, acquired the lease himself in 1860, developing the business extensively over the next decade. In 1890 he went into partnership with Lord Lothian to form the Lothian Coal Company which incorporated coalfields from Rosewell to Newtongrange.

Carnethie Street used to be known by a variety of names including Whitehill Place, Duke Street and Lindsay Place. Rosewell itself was known as 'Little Ireland' on account of its large number of immigrant Irish miners. A previous resident of Carnethie Street brought a court action against the village's Irish National Foresters Benefit Society. Before the welfare state, paying a regular stipend to a Benefit or Friendly Society was the only financial safety net in the event of sickness. Francis McCulloch sued his society when it refused to pay out when he was ill but it claimed that he hadn't sent in his medical certificates and its treasurer didn't believe he'd been to hospital.

Carnethie Street was one of the earliest places to be renovated as part of Rosewell's regeneration plan in the 1990s which involved road narrowing and landscaping. The origin of Rosewell's name isn't known exactly but one of the possibilities, that the village wells were surrounded by roses, seems likely if predictable. More likely, at least, than the hokum repeated by the Dalkeith Advertiser that an early encampment of soldiers in the district told their sergeant that they had 'rose well' on so many mornings that it just caught on... In 1952 Rosewell, as a typical mining village, was considered the perfect film location for John Grierson's "The Brave Don't Cry", based on the Knockshinnoch mining disaster. A decade later, however, Whitehill Pit closed ending - for the most part - the villages connection to the industry.

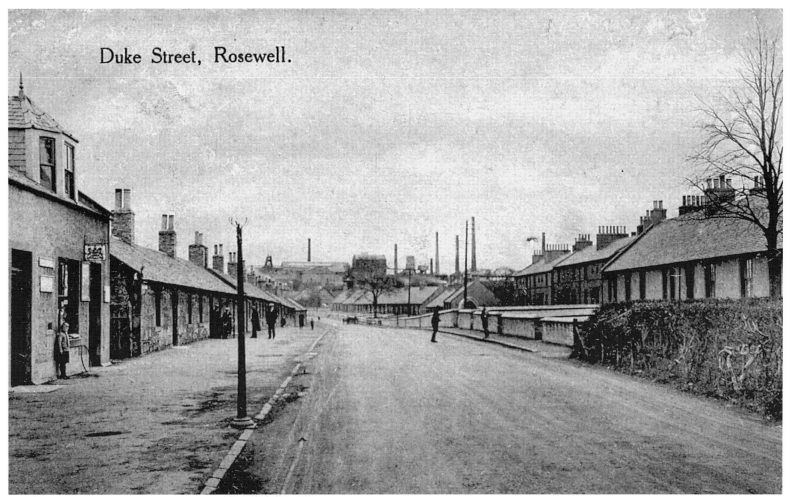

Duke Street, Rosewell.

Miners had a strong sense of community and in its heyday the workers at Whitehill pit could depend on support from the surrounding villages. In 1894 over one and a half thousand miners picketed Whitehill over a wage dispute. Men travelled from Gorebridge, Newtongrange and Newbattle to take part and many local women chose to attend the pithead over work at the local carpet factory. Around forty police were brought in to control the crowd although the Advertiser commented that there was little violence. The picket was successful and the Rosewell miners in turn gave their support to disputes elsewhere. A few days later the village miners marched to attend a picket at the Mauricewood Pit in Penicuik.

POST OFFICE, ROSEWELL.

Rosewell Post Office is still standing in this building. In fact, much of the village has remained the same and belies the devastation of the sixties and seventies. After Whitehill closed in 1961 men in the village lost their staple employment and their trade, unless they were willing to travel. The town's brickworks, symbol of its past success, also closed in the seventies. People began to leave to find work elsewhere and, like Newtongrange around the same time, Rosewell began to be labelled as a 'ghost town'. With no new building or industries moving into the area over the next decade it's a wonder that anyone was annoyed (and they were) when Councillor William Stoddart said at a meeting about Rosewell's future that the village was 'dying'.

Looking back up Carnethie Street, around 1908. After limping through the seventies Rosewell got a break, of sorts, when it was declared a Conservation Area in 1980. This involved the Local Authority taking over one hundred houses (about a third of the homes in the village) for renovation. Under this regime Rosewell was preserved as a mining village with residents needing permission from the council to make any changes such as putting up new buildings or planting trees. A mining revival came to the town briefly in 1994 when an opencast mine was built on the former site of the Whitehill Pit. Rosewell's regeneration programme picked up over the years, in an attempt to follow the success of Newtongrange. New building took place to increase the population and Carnethie Street, its main road, received a face-lift. A bypass was also built for the village to decrease traffic and make room for front gardens.

Rosewell's Miner's Institute, pictured here when it was still going strong, is just down from the Post Office. Taking a look at it today gives us a rather more sceptical view of the village's regeneration. In 1994 the club had four hundred members but it was suffering financial difficulties. Today, after eighty years, it is boarded up and derelict, with its windows smashed. The bypass, built on the site of a huge opencast mine, took away all the nasty traffic but whether or not that was a good move for a 'ghost town' is debatable. On top of all this some of Rosewell's newly renovated homes started to suffer massive subsidence in the mid-1990s on account of being built on old mine workings, although this was an old story in the town. A few decades earlier a three hundred and thirty-six foot shaft appeared at the entrance to the brickworks overnight.

Ramsay Hall, Rosewell.

813/5

The Ramsay Hall on the right missed out on Rosewell's Conservation Order by a long shot, being demolished in the fifties. Built on the site of the old village school, the 'Dame School', it was the oldest hall in Rosewell before its demise. The building was originally used for missionary purposes, something which was quite common in Scottish villages before 1900. Once churches opened in the area the mission work stopped and the hall was used for dances and events. At one point it also housed pupils of Rosewell school when it burned down.

Everything in this 1910 picture, and more, was either controlled or set up by the company; the Tavern, the shop, the police station, the PO and the houses. Even the Co-op, which was normally set up by a collective of interested locals, was instigated by Hood in 1861. Co-ops became popular during the nineteenth century as a way of coping with poverty and the high prices at the company shop, which could be the only grocery outlet available. Rosewell's Co-op was knocked down during the war and rebuilt on the same spot. The buildings on either side in this picture have gone and the Co-op itself has since been remodelled into a corner shop.

The Tavern, Rosewell.

ROSEWELL CO-OPERATIVE STORE, LIMITED.
ROSEWELL TAVERN

In the days before the Tavern men used to buy beer by the bucket at the Co-op which had a licence. The pub has survived as The Clenorie. The Co-op was originally next to the Hawthornden Inn which had a chequered past itself. The site started off as the Barn which was used for dances, weddings and even Catholic mass in the days before a Catholic church had appeared. This was demolished in 1925 and replaced with the pavilion for Rosedale Football Club. It was transformed again into a cafe before finally appearing as the Inn.

HAWTHORNDEN STATION.

Another absent facility, Hawthornden Station was extant in 1962 but is now long gone. The branch line opened in 1872 but since the rails were removed the trackbed forms a footpath instead to Auchendinny and Penicuik. In the nineties transport can be a problem but despite all the doom and gloom of its past Rosewell has its positive moments. The village may be quiet but, thanks to the Conservation Order, its streets are neat and well-kept. Some commentators have actually said that out of all the villages in the area Rosewell is the one which has retained its identity apart. But the villages crowning glory in recent years has to be Whitehill Welfare F.C.'s game against Celtic in the 1996 Scottish Cup. They lost 3-0 to the Glasgow supremos but half the population booked seats at the match and the story kept the local papers going for weeks.

Rosewell Primary, built some time before 1891, has been dramatically rebuilt, remodelled into a lovely modern 'box' shape. In the past Rosewell had a huge Catholic population made up of Irish, Lithuanians and Poles, and there were squabbles amongst the authorities over the establishment of an R.C. school. One of the main protesters missed out on the final vote in the 1890s causing his rivals to snigger that 'Providence must be a Roman Catholic!". A century later the big Catholic story in the village regarded the Venerable Margaret Sinclair, who was up for canonisation. St. Margaret's Chapel in the village apparently had her 'relics' and the papers did a round of articles on her 'miracles'. Jimmy Saville, of all people, got involved when it came to light that his mother had prayed to her when he was ill as a child.

I've been told the Hoods once resided at Rosedale House. The mansion still stands today but it is extremely unlikely that anyone will have noticed as it is completely obscured by a hedge of 'Sleeping Beauty' proportions. Whatever Hood was like as a boss, he certainly didn't have it easy. In 1890 Alexander Blair of Duke Street took out a court action against him for negligence. His twelve year old son Henry had a leg amputated after an accident at the colliery railway although Hood claimed that he couldn't be held responsible. The following year he was accused of underhand methods during a pit dispute, a cause which was taken up by Mr Haldane, MP for East Lothian at the time. The colliery manager wanted men down his mines for nine hours instead of eight. Hood had apparently fobbed of officials sent to investigate, claiming predictably that it was only a few trouble-makers who complained.